FABULOUS HAIR

Written by Maria Neuman
Photography by Angela Coppola

LONDON, NEW YORK, MUNICH,
MELBOURNE, AND DELHI

Editor Elizabeth Hester
Designer Jee Chang
Managing Art Editor Michelle Baxter
Art Director Dirk Kaufman
Publishing Director Beth Sutinis
Lead Illustrator Jeremy Canceko
Additional Illustrations Matt Dicke,
Paul Hoppe, Engly Cheng, Erin Harney
Production Ivor Parker
DTP Design Kathy Farias

Produced by Downtown Bookworks Inc.
President: Julie Merberg
Director: Patty Brown
Editor: Sarah Parvis

Freelance Beauty Editor JoanneNoel Higgins
Photographer Angela Coppola

First published in Great Britain in 2006 by
Dorling Kindersley Limited
80 Strand, London WC2R ORL

06 07 08 09 10 10 9 8 7 6 5 4 3 2 1

A catalogue record for this book is available
from the British Library.

ISBN: 1-4053-1458-3

Color reproduction by Colourscan, Singapore
Printed and bound in China by
South China Printing Co., Ltd.

Discover more at
www.dk.com

contents

What's Your Haircare IQ?

Hairstyles for School

Hairstyles for the Weekend

Party-Time Hair!

Alexis

What is your haircare IQ?

Just like your face or your feet, your hair is unique to you. In this book, we're here to show you that no matter what length, texture or type, there are lots of cool styles out there that are right for you – from the quick updo before P.E. class to a funky bun for shopping or a glam-o-rama French twist for a fancy party. As well as creating exciting styles, you will also learn to take care of your locks and keep them looking their best. With some simple steps and key products, this will be a breeze. So, are you ready for some serious hair education? Need to know the difference between gel and mousse? How to make that updo work for you or the styling secrets to accessorising with pizzazz? *Fabulous Hair* has you covered!

What is your hair type?

Before you can start styling up a storm, it's helpful to figure out exactly what type of hair you have. It can make a huge difference in how a style looks on you, as well as what type of styling products you should use. Check out the pictures and descriptions of the girls on these pages, and match yourself to the one (or ones) who looks most like you. Then watch out for her picture throughout the book – she'll have specialised style tips just for you!

handy tips

style tip
If you've got a fringe, just twist it back in Step 2 and secure it with a couple of slides above your ears.

Watch out for these tip boxes throughout the book – the girls will have some great tips for every hair type.

These symbols at the beginning of each style will give you an idea of how much time it will take to create.

Hair pro or beginner? One solid bar means a style is easy; four means it's pretty tricky. Take your pick.

Alexis

Hi, I'm Alexis! If your hair is long, medium thick, and straight like mine, you probably have many of the same issues as me, like…

- My hair can look flat and stringy sometimes.

- I can curl my hair with hot rollers but it won't stay in place unless I use some styling products.

- My hair can look oily if I don't wash it everyday.

- My hair gets flyaway in dry weather.

- Any type of volumizing product like mousse or gel looks great in my hair.

Nikki

My name is Nikki. I love my dark hair colour and great shine. I have fine hair but it can look thick because I have a lot of it. Fine hair can be tricky to style because it just wants to lie flat. Is this you?:

- With fine hair, even a ponytail can look wimpy.

- Even with gel and curlers, my style will only last a few hours.

- I need lots of hair spray to keep an updo in place.

- I like to wash my hair every day – otherwise it will look really flat and greasy.

- Light products like gel and mousse work on my hair but heavier stuff like creams and waxes just weigh it down.

Rosie

Amy

Nierah

My name is Rosie. All my friends say they wish they had my curls, but this hair can drive me crazy! Do you go through this?

- My hair gets frizzy in the rain or humidity.

- With any sleek style I need to straighten my hair first.

- My hair can only be kept under control with lots of leave-in conditioner and straightening creams.

- Wax is great for separating my hair.

- I don't need to wash my hair everyday because it's a bit dry.

I'm Amy. My hair is thick and a little bit wavy, and I've got a long fringe. I like my hair just hanging down, but sometimes it's a little tricky in an updo. Is this you?

- If it's humid outside, my hair gets frizzy.

- A curling iron works great on my hair as long as I use gel before and spray after.

- Since my hair is thick, I can skip a day of shampooing because it never looks flat.

- If I start blowdrying my hair when it's too wet it will take forever. Slightly damp works best.

- My hair gets flyaway when the weather is dry and cold.

My name is Nierah. Short hair like mine can be fun and easy but it can also be limiting. My hair is coarse, which makes it perfect for updos because it stays in place well. Does this sound like you?

- My hair is great at holding a curl, but since it's dry I have to be careful using the curling iron or any other heated styling gadgets.

- I can skip the shampoo a couple of days in a row but I always need to condition my dry ends.

- Light products like gel and mousse are drying on my hair. I need leave-in conditioners and styling creams.

- My hair can get flyaway when the weather is very dry.

Found your hair-type partner?
Time to style!

styling**stuff**

Hair is beautiful naturally, but making it look great in a style takes a little help from the right products. Remember this rule of thumb: The finer your hair, the lighter your products should be. Fine-haired girls should stick to a misting of light hairspray or a puff of mousse. Thick or curly hair can take a heavier wax or gel. No matter what type you choose, be careful not to overdo it – the only way to take product out is to hit the shower! Read on to see how to achieve your style goals.

clean and condition

shampoo, conditioner,
leave-in conditioner

If your hair is oily, wash it every day. Girls with curls usually have drier hair, so you can easily skip a day. Shampoo right down to your roots – but avoid putting too much conditioner right on your scalp as it can make hair look limp.

smooth and straighten
wax, shine spray

If you're plugging in straighteners, make sure to spritz each piece of hair with a straightening spray to keep it protected. Waxes add a messy, textured edge to all styles but should only be used sparingly.

volumize
mousse, gel

Listen up fine-haired females: mousse works great on damp hair and should be applied from roots to ends. A volumizing gel should just go on the roots because it's a little thicker.

hold
gel, hairspray

EVERYONE needs a good hairspray. If you're creating an updo, it's always the final touch. A quick spray over the whole head will keep everything in place.

how much?
To avoid looking frizzy or over-slicked, be sure to use the right amount.

A pea-sized amount of product is good for heavy stuff like wax.

A medium-sized amount is great for leave-in conditioner, styling cream or gel.

A tennis ball-sized amount is right for fluffy stuff like mousse.

tool school

The number one trick to creating the hairstyles in this book is to have the right tools. Not quite sure which gadget does what? We've rounded up the most common items (and the ones you'll need to do the looks in here) and explained what each one does and any tips you need to know when buying your own.

hot stuff

These are the stylers that dry, straighten or crimp your hair. They can get seriously hot, so always use them with care.

A crimping iron has two interlocking zig-zag plates. To use it, squeeze a section of hair between the two plates for about five seconds, then move down the hair shaft.

A curling iron is the fastest way to add curl. Choose a wider barrel for a looser curl or a narrow one for ringlets. Whatever size you chooose, only let hair set about 5–7 seconds at a time.

A good blowdryer makes drying time faster and also helps lessen frizz. Look for one that has both hot and cold settings and a nozzle attachment to direct the air and downplay frizz.

A diffuser attachment disperses air so it doesn't come out of the hairdryer in one huge blast (making curls a tangled mess).

Velcro rollers are another way to get curls. They have Velcro teeth to grip hair and stay in place, but you need a blow dryer to heat and dry the hair.

Hot rollers are best when you want princess-like curls all over your head. They need about 10 minutes to preheat and are secured onto your head with special pins.

Straighteners get hair poker straight. They're made of two metal or ceramic plates that work just like irons. To use, clamp them at the top of a section of hair. Then drag them down the hair to the ends.

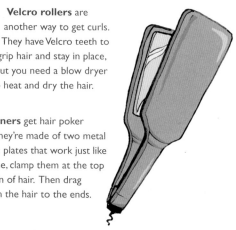

Brushes and combs

Not only do brushes and combs get the tangles out, they are also the perfect styling partners for heat stylers or products.

A wide-tooth comb is best for combing wet or damp hair to get the tangles out. These are also good for combing through gel or mousse products evenly.

A round brush is what you need for blow-drying hair straight. The brush can be used from below while a blowdryer heats from above. It can also be used to curl ends.

A paddle brush has a flat surface with bristles popping out. It's best for brushing dry hair.

A fine-tooth comb is great for making a parting in your hair and also for smoothing down a style when you're finished – a spritz of hairspray and a light combing with this tool will leave your style perfect.

Pins and clips

Finally, no style will stay put without an array of pins, clips and elastics. Trust us, you can never have too many.

Slides are great for securing loose pieces to a tricky updo or pulling strands back from your face. Just open it up between fingers and slip it in. A hair grip is already open, and is better for fastening sections of a bun or twist into place.

hair slide   **hair grip**

Crocodile clips come in small or large sizes – just pinch the back pieces together to open it up and then clamp it down over the hair. The big ones can hold a ponytail, but the mall ones are best for decoration or holding tiny twists of hair.

Hair elastics are fantastic. If you have fine hair choose smaller ones, whereas thicker hair can handle the thicker styles. They also come in different sizes, so pick the right size for your style.

10 tips for really healthy hair

Strong, shiny hair is the best foundation for any style. To keep your tresses looking their best, you need to learn how to care for your scalp and hair. That means nourishing, protecting and grooming your locks. Be good to your hair and it will love you back!

1 **Get regular trims:** Even if you're growing your hair, get it snipped every 3–6 months to keep the ends from splitting.

2 **Lather up:** If your hair is oily, wash it every day. If your hair is on the dryer side, feel free to skip a day.

3 **Water works:** If you're a pool princess, always rinse your hair with water after swimming to get rid of chlorine, which can fry hair and make blond locks look green.

4 **Detangling tricks:** Always use a wide-tooth comb to detangle your hair right after a shower.

5 **Elastic alert:** Don't use regular rubber bands to put your hair up. Use snag-free hair elastics to avoid breaks and split ends.

6

Food for thought: You hair is a reflection of what you eat, so make sure to keep it looking good by eating lots of fruit, vegetables and lean protein (chicken and fish).

7

Product pick: You should only use two styling products at one time. If you need more to keep a style in place, it's probably not the right 'do for you.

8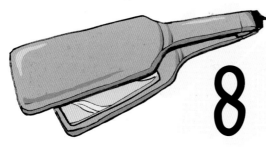

Hot hot hot: If you're unsure, ask a stylist to show you how to use a straightening or curling iron. If used incorrectly they can seriously fry your style.

9

Hey, Sunshine! Hair gets sunburned just like your skin. Comb a dollop of sunscreen or leave-in conditioner through before you go to the beach.

10

Frizz factor: One of the main causes of frizz is rubbing wet hair with a towel to get it dry. Instead, just blot or squeeze it using a towel.

top10 hair basics

The type of style you want depends on what type of hair accessory you use. For example, a butterfly crocodile clip gives a totally different vibe than a flowery slide. This is where you can really show your flair for fashion as well as keeping your style in place. Below, we've rounded up 10 favourite hair treats, as well as telling you what to do with them and who they're best for.

1 **Headbands** are great for keeping hair off the face or spicing up a low ponytail.

3 **Slides** can be decoration while also holding your hair in place at the same time – genius!

2 **Hairpins** are great for securing a bun in place – with the added flowers they're really pretty.

4 **Clips are cute** to hold back a growing-out fringe. Why not get some with attached ribbons in your school colours?

5

These chopsticks can hold a bun in place on their own, or just stick into a finished updo for a little Asian flavor.

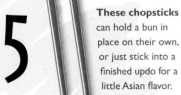

6

These snag-free elastics are safe for hair because they don't have any metal joints. Plus, you can mix and match the colors to go with your outfit.

7

These skinny elastic headbands are great for pulling your hair off your face in class. They look cool just wrapped around your wrist, too.

Crocodile clips are perfect for keeping twists or plaits from unravelling. Bigger versions can hold a whole ponytail in place. Just snap one on right at the scalp for a quick grip.

8

9

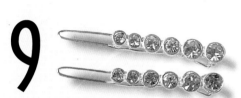

Baby clips are the perfect decoration for a fancy updo or when you just want to add some sparkle to your hair.

10

Combs like this are the accessory equivalent of tucking your hair behind your ears. They work best on thicker hair.

How do you wear your hair to school?

You know the drill: The alarm goes off and it's time for another school day. It doesn't take much effort to look for a fresh outfit every day, but hair can be a little trickier. Do you ever feel stuck in a style rut and end up just throwing your hair back into the same old ponytail? You're not alone. But there is help! The following pages are full of schoolday styles that can be created in minutes. You'll find enough variety to whip up new looks all week, and they're all P.E. tested and won't fall in your face during that crucial maths test. So check out these super-cute 'dos, find your favourites, and get styling! You'll look so great from the neck up that no one would notice even if you were wearing the same clothes two days in a row.

ziggityzaggity

Here's a quick and cool way to make your hair look funky even when it's just hanging loose. With a couple of quick turns of a comb it's simple to turn your basic centre parting into this jagged look. This is the perfect style to try if you've only got a few minutes before catching the school bus, because the Ziggity Zaggity only takes a minute.

how to do it

you'll need: comb • hair spray

1 Start by combing damp hair using a wide-tooth comb. Comb your hair forwards, so the sides fall in your face.

2 Take the comb and starting from the back of your head (right at the crown, where your natural parting starts), drag the comb forward in a diagonal line about 2 cm. Separate your hair with your hands as you go.

3 Switch to the opposite diagonal direction and go 2 cm that way. Continue switching back and forth until you reach the front of your head.

mix it up!

zig zag style alert

OK, now that you've mastered the Ziggity Zaggity parting, it's time to do something with the rest of your hair. To really showcase that parting, pick a style that sits low (like a ponytail, pigtail or bun), and smooth hair back to give the parting centre stage.

style tip

If you have fine hair, spritz on shine spray or leave-in conditioner to tame flyaway strands and keep your zigzag parting looking clean and crisp.

dress it up!

These clips prove that it's hip to be square!

A flowery slide helps finish your smooth look in the prettiest way.

Decorative twists give this look a playful spin when they're placed at the corners of the parting.

A butterfly elastic is a pretty addition to any ponytail, and the bright yellow colour draws attention to simple styles.

messy**pony**

This is an easy way to make your favourite style a little funkier. The best part is that since it's supposed to be less than perfect, it's one of the few 'dos that's hard to do "wrong"! It actually works better on hair that isn't squeaky clean, so try this on a day when you haven't washed your hair, or as an easy updo after a busy day.

how to do it

you'll need: blowdryer • wide-tooth comb • hair elastic • wax

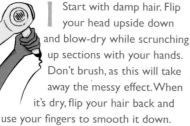

1 Start with damp hair. Flip your head upside down and blow-dry while scrunching up sections with your hands. Don't brush, as this will take away the messy effect. When it's dry, flip your hair back and use your fingers to smooth it down.

2 Grab your hair with both hands and pull it back into a loose ponytail. Use an elastic to fasten. The best place for your ponytail is right in the middle of your head, in the back.

3 Rub a pea-sized amount of wax in your hands. Next, grab sections of your ponytail and massage the wax into them one section at a time to create even more of a crazy, messy, cool look.

curly girls

If you're blessed with beautiful ringlets, place your ponytail a little lower and looser for a romantic look. The looser your ponytail, the more your curls will show – try placing the hair elastic in a few different locations until you find the one you like.

dress it up!

A beaded elastic has more drama than your average ponytail holder – but works just the same.

Decorative pins can transform a messy pony into an elegant 'do for special occasions.

A row of mini crocodile clips adds an extra accent.

Flowing ribbons fit the casual romantic mood of a low, loose ponytail.

style tip

A bit of mousse can help plump up fine hair to get the fullness and body that look great in this style.

looped**bunches**

Feeling a little loopy? Then this style is perfect for you! These simple bunches have been turned up and tucked under. Not only is this style easy to do, but it can also look cute and dressy if you just add the right accessory. If you're keeping it casual, we think it's great for keeping hair out of your face in P.E. too!

how to do it

you'll need: brush • 2 hair elastics

1 Brush your hair so it's knot-free. The use the end of a comb to divide it down the middle.

2 Gather one side into a bunch and start securing it with a elastic. On the final wrap of the elastic, simply stop short of pulling the bunch all the way through.

3 When you've got both bunches looped, adjust them with your hands so that they are the same size.

plait fantastic

If your hair is crazy curly, these bunches might not work for you. To keep it sleek, put your hair into bunches, plait it, and secure with an elastic at the bottom. Then bend the end of the plait underneath and pin it where it meets the top.

Hide the ends of your hair under a big ribbon or choose one that's already attached to an elastic.

dress it up!

Use these cool textured elastics for some added colour.

A shimmery flower elastic makes this funky style look dressed up.

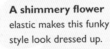

Pale pink coral clips are a sweet way to pin back a fringe or stray pieces.

baby**twists**

If you love to wear your hair down but still want to add a little personality, this style is for you. These twists look just as cute from the front as from the back, and they're pretty on all types of hair. Got long layers? Try using this style as a fresh way to keep hair out of your face for schooldays.

how to do it

you'll need: brush • comb • elastic

1 Brush your hair so that it is knot-free. Give yourself a straight centre parting using the end of a comb.

2 Take two small sections from the front of your head (either side of your center parting). Divide each section into 2 pieces and tightly cross one section over the other section until you reach the end. Secure with an elastic band.

3 Join the two pieces at the back of your head with one elastic (take out the ones holding the 2 twists secure).

dress it up!

A shimmery clip clamps flat over hair and comes in pretty shades like iridescent pink.

This clip can be worn with the metal part tucked under hair so only the flower shows. Cute!

Polka-dot crocodile clips are cool for school days and casual weekends, too.

Put a clip in to keep twists in place.

twisty chick

If you're feeling really creative, try doing four twists instead of two. Just follow the original steps, except for Step 2, where you will take four sections instead of two. To keep it simple, do the two original plaits first (Step 3) and then add the second pair.

style tip

Trying to grow out your fringe? This is the perfect style for you.

knottygirls

Not only is this one of our favourite school styles (it's funky and functional), but once you master knots, you can add them to a bunch of different styles. Think of it like tying a knot in a piece of string. Also, if you've got a shorter 'do, this style is adaptable — so now you and your best friend can sport the same style but still look totally different!

how to do it

you'll need: comb • gel • 3 hair elastics

1 Using the end of a comb, divide the front of your hair into three sections (left side, top, and right side). Rub a tiny bit of gel between your hands and smooth your hands over the sections of hair. Secure each section at the base, by your scalp, with a small elastic.

2 Grab one section and twist it around into a coil. Next, take the coil and tie it into a knot and then push the knot down until it is around the elastic.

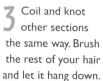

3 Coil and knot other sections the same way. Brush the rest of your hair and let it hang down.

short-haired knots

Shorter hair can be hard to tie into this style.
To imitate the look without getting crazy-looking
sprouts, try making knots or twists with smaller
sections of hair. Try a bunch of small knots above
your forehead or line up some twists along the
side of your head.

dress it up!

A hard plastic flower is a fitting end for vine-like twists.

Add a Hawaiian punch with a hibiscus slide.

These twist-in gems will add sparkle right next to the knots.

Matching pink slides and elastics? Totally cute.

style tip

If your hair is curly, it's easier to create these knots while your hair is still damp to avoid tangles.

funky**bunches**

Put a funky twist to a simple style. Whether you're at school or out shopping, this look is sweet and simple. We love it because it's easy to alter and is the perfect way to show off all our favourite colours with lots of elastics. (Add as many as you want – you can never have too many.) A perfect combination of cool and colourful!

how to do it
you'll need: comb • hair elastics (at least six)

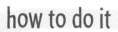

1 Start by combing out damp hair using a wide-tooth comb. Next, take the end of the comb and make a centre parting. Secure both sections with elastics into two low bunches.

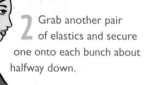

2 Grab another pair of elastics and secure one onto each bunch about halfway down.

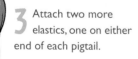

3 Attach two more elastics, one on either end of each pigtail.

add a plait

For a special twist on this funky style, plait the hair between the elastics. You can loop the last section to add even more interest. It's a pretty way to keep your hair out of the way for sports and to stay super-cool on summer days.

mix it up!

These hip elastics have pretty beading.

style tip

Girls with short hair can move the elastics closer together or use two instead of three.

dress it up!

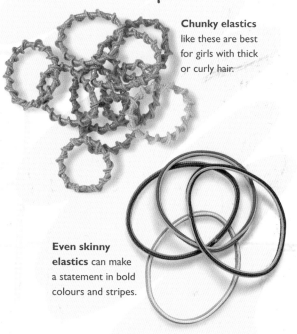

Chunky elastics like these are best for girls with thick or curly hair.

Even skinny elastics can make a statement in bold colours and stripes.

sporty**pony**

Need to look athletic and stylish at the same time? This is the look for you! It pulls all of your hair off your face and neck, so it's perfect for any sport from gymnastics to track. Also, check out our way of showing off your school colours by adding co-ordinating accessories. If you're on a team, show everyone this style so you can all take the lead in the style game!

how to do it

you'll need: wide-tooth comb • hair elastics

1 Detangle damp hair using a wide-tooth comb (this will help this style to look really smooth and sleek). Then, gather the hair from the top and side of your head and secure with an elastic just below the crown of your head.

style tip

If you want to use decorative ponytail holders on top of plain elastics, remember to add them as you go.

2 Gather about another third of your hair, pulling from the sides and the area just below the first ponytail. Secure with an elastic about 5 cm above your hairline.

dress it up!

Make this style less sporty and more pretty by adding a flower.

3 Now gather up all your hair and secure it into a low ponytail. Girls with longer hair can add another ponytail holder lower down, like the Funky Bunches.

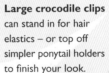

Cool textures like faux suede make the most of this style. Pick colours that contrast with your hair to make them stand out.

Large crocodile clips can stand in for hair elastics – or top off simpler ponytail holders to finish your look.

low**pigtails**

We love the look of pigtails and being able to make a plait opens up all sorts of hairstyle possibilities! Since this look is all about casual, keep your accessories the same – skip the rhinestones and think flowers, shells or try wrapping a bandana around your head instead!

how to do it

you'll need: blowdryer • brush • comb • hair elastics

1 Blowdry your hair until it is completely dry. Brush to de-tangle your dry hair. Next, use the end of a comb to divide your hair along a centre parting. Put one side into a loose bunch to get it out of the way.

2 Carefully divide the loose side into three sections. Begin plaiting by crossing the righthand piece over the middle piece, then the lefthand piece over the middle piece. Repeat until you reach the end of the pigtail, then secure with an elastic.

3 Now take the second side out of the bunch and repeat Step 2 to make another plait. Once both plaits are finished, adjust the ponytail holders to be sure they look even. You're done!

dress it up!

This hair elastic will add a little petal power to the end of any plait.

A bright ribbon brings this look some girlish charm. Use two of the same colour or mix and match.

A woolly hat tops this look in wintertime. The plaits are smooth enough to fit under a fitted cap, and look adorable sticking out the bottom.

style tip

If your hair is too short to stay neatly tucked into plaits, pin the loose pieces back with a clip or slide – or let the pieces fall for a style that's messy-chic.

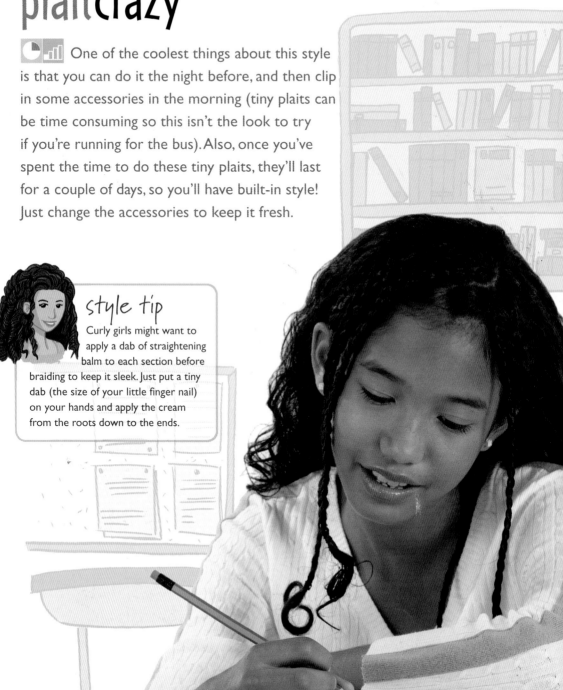

plait**crazy**

One of the coolest things about this style is that you can do it the night before, and then clip in some accessories in the morning (tiny plaits can be time consuming so this isn't the look to try if you're running for the bus). Also, once you've spent the time to do these tiny plaits, they'll last for a couple of days, so you'll have built-in style! Just change the accessories to keep it fresh.

style tip

Curly girls might want to apply a dab of straightening balm to each section before braiding to keep it sleek. Just put a tiny dab (the size of your little finger nail) on your hands and apply the cream from the roots down to the ends.

how to do it

you'll need: brush • small hair elastics

1 Brush your hair so that it is knot-free. Take small 2 cm square sections of hair (make about five) and secure them loosely with elastics. It's a good idea to pull the rest of your hair into a loose ponytail to get it out of the way while you're plaiting.

2 Take the elastic out of one piece of hair and divide the piece into three sections. Begin plaiting by crossing the righthand section over the middle section and then the lefthand section over the middle section. Repeat until you reach the end of your hair and secure with an elastic.

3 Plait the rest of the sections of hair around your face, take the back of your hair out of the ponytail and give it one last brush.

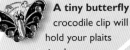
dress it up!

A tiny butterfly crocodile clip will hold your plaits in place.

Mini crocodile clips can hold a few plaits together.

Clip plaits into a bunch with a flowery clip or this rhinestone sparkle clip.

Use a tiny clip to gather plaits for a more polished look.

simple sophistication

To change this style from fun to finished: Instead of keeping all the plaits at the front of your head, distribute them along your part and then gather the mini-plaits at the side of your head.

mix it up!

rope**plaits**

OK, so you know how to do a basic plait. Are you ready to take it to the next level? Try the rope plait. It's actually easier than a regular plait because hair is only divided into two sections instead of three. Also, we give you two different ways to wear the Rope Plait here – but why not try your own ideas? Do as many as you want and see how you like it.

how to do it

you'll need: brush • 2 elastics

1 Brush dry hair back into a ponytail and secure it with an elastic.

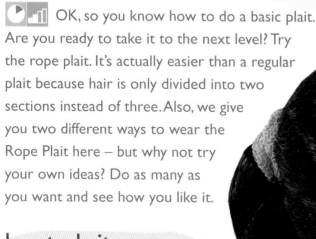

2 Separate the ponytail into two equal sections.

3 Tightly cross one section over the other section until you reach the end of your ponytail and secure it with an elastic.

the baby rope

How cute is this? Instead of a regular plait at the side of your face, why not mix it up every once in a while with a mini Rope Plait. Secure it with a cute elastic or clip and you've got a great new look!

A twisty elastic mimics the texture of the plait. Cool!

mix it up!

style tip

If you've got a fringe, try the Baby Rope a little further back. It will look good coming from the hair right behind your fringe.

dress it up!

Copy our lovely lavender look with one purple scrunchy at the top and one at the bottom of the rope plait.

These elastics are covered in beads. So pretty!

Girls with thick hair can add some hair gems into the rope plait.

chicchignon

Whether you're at school or surfing the web this cool twist is what you need. This is the type of style that looks cool all day – then, with a couple of tweaks and added accessories, it can easily be ready to party. That means you don't have to spend an hour in the mirror trying to create your hairstyle and you can use all that extra time planning the perfect outfit instead!

how to do it

you'll need: 2 elastics • hairspray • hair slides • shine spray

1 Gather dry hair into a ponytail at the back of your head. Make sure the top and sides look really smooth and sleek.

style tip
If your hair is on the shorter side, create this style while your hair is damp. Massage a medium-sized dab of gel into the hair by starting with your roots and working your gel coated hands down to the ends. Now you can comb hair back and start with Step 1.

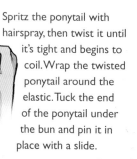

2 Spritz the ponytail with hairspray, then twist it until it's tight and begins to coil. Wrap the twisted ponytail around the elastic. Tuck the end of the ponytail under the bun and pin it in place with a slide.

3 Pin the rest of the bun in place by grabbing hair from your scalp and the bun at the same time (this will make it feel budge proof). Spritz your whole head lightly with a shine spray to make it look very glossy and glam.

dress it up!

This tortoiseshell accessory can be secured over the bun for a whole new look.

Hair combs look great stuck on either side of the bun (so the teeth go into the bun) for a little added drama.

A hair pin with a giant flower is the perfect partytime addition to the Chic Chignon.

Nikki

Alexis

How do you wear your hair on the weekend?

Time to ditch your school books and get ready to have some fun. What are you doing this weekend? Going shopping with your friends, having a sleepover or just chilling out with your family? Weekends are all about having a good time and we've got some cool 'dos that will suit your mood no matter what you've got planned. You'll find ideas for every hair type as well as easy-to-follow tips on working a bandana, mastering pretty hair jewels and the newest flower hair accessories. Why not get together will your friends and have fun trying out these hairstyles on each other? Be sure to have some supplies on hand – pins, clips, ribbons, and lots of imagination!

pickabunch

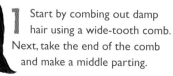 Bunches might be super simple, but that doesn't mean they have to be boring. Check out these cool ideas for adding a little pizzazz to a favourite style. Are you feeling a little bit hippie? Add a bandana. Go girly by placing bunches high on your head. Whatever you choose, be sure to add some personality to this funky style to make it truly your own.

how to do it
you'll need: comb • 2 elastics

1 Start by combing out damp hair using a wide-tooth comb. Next, take the end of the comb and make a middle parting.

2 Brush one section of your hair into a low bunch, securing it behind your ear with a hair elastic. Do the same on the other side.

3 Finish the look by knotting a bandana under the bunches. You can match the bandana to the elastics or mix it up – it's up to you!

dress it up!

With this cute cap, hat hair is a very good thing.

This pretty ribbon is small enough to be subtle, but is really colourful

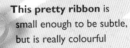

style tip

A fringe can do a disappearing act in this style – or take centre stage. Let them hang normally for a funky vibe, or move the bandana up to hold them back and out of sight.

A ring of flowers draws extra attention to pretty bunches.

A pink plastic bow tops this elastic.

mix it up!

aim high!

If you're more of a girlie girl, skip the scarf and place your bunches really high. Secure them with your favourite pink accessory for an added feminine touch. This style also looks fabulous if you have curly hair.

toptwist

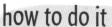 This funky and functional style keeps your hair out of your face and is perfect for a day with your friends. The number of twists you do is up to you; it's easy to do fewer if you're short for time — just use our idea as a suggestion. You can also have loads of fun choosing accessories.

how to do it

you'll need: a comb • gel • hairspray
• 3 medium crocodile clips • at least 9 mini crocodile clips

1 Start by combing damp hair with a wide tooth comb. When it's knot-free, comb all your hair straight backwards from your forehead – this will make it easier to part.

2 Use your comb to divide your hair into left-side, top, and right-side sections, securing each piece with a crocodile clip to keep your hair separated.

3 Remove clip from one section and at the hairline, select about half of that section to work with. Start twisting your hair backwards with your fingers, picking up more hair the further back you go. After a few inches, use a mini crocodile clip to secure the twist.

4 Repeat Step 3 until you've replaced all three big crocodile clips with two or three little twists each. Line up the mini crocodile clips so they're all in a row, then spritz your head lightly with hairspray and pat down any stray hairs.

dress it up!

Use slides instead of clips for a different look. They can criss-cross or line up to look like a headband.

Pick crocodile clips in a bunch of cool colours and patterns.

With colourful elastics, you can wear the back of your hair in a ponytail instead of down. Match them up to the clips and you'll look really co-ordinated.

style tip

If your hair doesn't like to lie smooth, rub a medium-sized dollop of gel through damp hair before you start twisting.

flirty**flick**

This style gives the classic blow-out a kick. With the sides smooth and sleek, it's a great way to show off pretty hair ornaments – or you can wear it loose. It takes some styling stuff to keep this 'do all day, but even if the "flick" part falls, your locks should keep the polished look.

how to do it

you'll need: hair gel • straighteners • blowdryer • round brush • wide-tooth comb • 6 large crocodile clips

1 Start with damp hair. Massage a medium-sized dollop of gel from roots to ends. Comb your hair to remove tangles, then use the comb to make a side parting from the crown of your head and forward. Divide your hair into six sections (three top and three bottom), twisting and clamping each section with a crocodile clip.

2 Section by section, begin blow-drying your hair straight. Use a round brush on the underside of the section, pulling hair down from roots to tips with the hairdryer blowing right above it. Keep your hair taut. Repeat this until section is smooth, then move onto the next section.

3 Now for the "flick": Spritz ends with hairspray. When your straighteners are hot, clamp them a few inches above the bottom of your hair, flip them up (away from hair), and drag them to the ends. Continue flicking as many sections as you like.

dress it up!

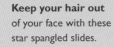

Hair gems look great attached right next to your parting.

Add these star clips on the side to add a bit of shine.

Keep your hair out of your face with these star spangled slides.

Be beachy keen by using these shell hair grips to clip up your flicks.

style tip

To all you curly girls, it's totally possible to get your hair poker straight but it takes time – the curlier the hair the longer you will have to repeat Step 2.

so cute!

Flicks are adorable on shorter hair because it looks a bit retro (think 1950's). Try them with a middle parting and use a little shine spray so your hair really gleams.

pigtail twist

When it comes to hairstyles, this pigtail twist combines a bunch of them. It's got pigtails, plaits, and a cool twisted bun, all in a funky style that looks amazing, especially on long and thick hair. It's also a perfect example of what can happen when you get creative. Wrap up this style with some pretty flowers, and you will really blossom!

mix it up!

double up!

Instead of creating one plait in each pigtail, make a couple of separate ones. When you loop the plaits around the base make sure to leave the ends of the plaits sticking out for an extra funky edge.

how to do it

you'll need: paddle brush • comb • elastic • slide • wax

1 Brush out dry hair to get rid of tangles. Using a comb, create a centre parting from the front of your forehead all the way back to the bottom of your hairline. Secure each section in a low ponytail right behind your ear.

2 Divide each bunch into three sections and plait. (Follow the steps on page 34 for creating basic plaits.)

3 On each side, wind the plait around the base of the ponytail to make a bun. Tuck the ends underneath, then secure the plait by pushing slides through the plait and towards the scalp and centre of the bun.

dress it up!

This orchid grip will hold any twist in place.

Tiny rhinestones give this slide a princess edge.

Hold down any stray hair with this dragonfly grip.

style tip

If you want the ends to stick out, add a dab of wax to make them spiky.

get with the band

Whether your hair is long or short, slipping in a colourful strip of fabric always looks good (it's also great for keeping that growing-out fringe out of your face). The style we've created here is all about blowdrying your hair straight so your wraparound band can really stand out. Remember, this is not the time to be shy with colour – be bold, bright and beautiful.

how to do it

you'll need: straightening balm • shine spray • wide-tooth comb • 6 big crocodile clips • blowdryer • round brush

1 Rub your hands together and distribute the balm throughout your hair, starting at the roots and working your way down to the ends. Comb your hair to remove tangles, then use the comb to divide your hair into six sections (three top and three bottom), twisting and clamping each section with a crocodile clip.

2 Section by section, begin by blowdrying your hair straight. Use a round brush on the underside of the section, pulling it down from roots to tips with the hairdryer blowing right above it. Keep your hair taut. Repeat this until the section is smooth, then move onto the next section.

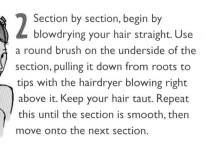

3 Mist your hair with shine spray and brush out. Slide in your headband in a smooth motion. For a cute pouf at the front, just push the headband forward an inch or so after it's placed.

dress it up!

This classic tortoiseshell headband has small teeth to keep your hair in place.

Fun, colourful elastic headbands look great if you wear a couple at a time.

style tip

Headbands look just as cute with curls. Just be sure to use shine spray or gel so frizz won't distract from this sophisticated style.

more band ideas

Don't think that you can only use headbands. Experiment with bandanas, your favourite ribbon or even a strip of an old T-shirt. Got a long scarf? Try using it as a headband and tying it around hair to make a ponytail. Now there's an accessory that's twice as nice!

A retro scarf will always look cool!

pool bunches

On your marks, get set, go! If you're at a pool party and about to take the plunge, don't forget to put up your hair in this water-friendly style. Not only do these 'dos keep your hair out of your face during a game of Marco Polo, the leave-in conditioner will also stop your style from getting seriously dried out from the chlorine.

how to do it

you'll need: leave-in conditioner
• wide-tooth comb • 4 hair elastics

1 Spritz damp hair with a leave-in conditioner spray. Brush out using a wide-tooth comb and create a centre parting that goes all the way from your forehead to the nape of your neck, so that hair is divided in two.

2 Take the right side of your hair and comb it again so it's really smooth. Secure it with an elastic into a high bunch. Do the same with the other side.

3 Gently twist one pigtail until it begins to coil. Make a loose knot, pulling the end of the pigtail through the loop. Secure with an elastic and repeat on the other side.

4 Give ends a tug so they sprout out the top, and you're ready to make a splash!

dress it up!

This plastic flower on an elastic is perfectly waterproof.

Be bold by using different coloured elastics.

Be a mermaid beauty and slip in some clips with rhinestones.

A terry-textured elastic is pool-perfect.

plait it

This variation is especially great for girls with longer hair: Just add plaits to your bunches before twisting, and you've got a cool style that will go swimmingly!

style tip

After swimming, remember to rinse your hair with regular water to flush out the chlorine.

prettyplaits

You already know that plaits are a great look but when you add a dash of colour they become even better! Preparing for this style can be a creative activity in itself as you pick out your favourite ribbons. You'll want to try this look again and again as you find new colours and textures. You can even try a bunch of different coloured ribbons at the same time for one very festive head!

style tip

If your hair is short, only make the plaits as long as you can before hair starts sticking out. A plait that only goes half way down the hair will still look great.

how to do it

you'll need: brush • elastic • ribbon

1 Start with dry hair and brush it to remove tangles. Grab a 2 cm square section of hair from the front and secure it with a tiny elastic about a little way down from the roots. Now take a thin ribbon that is twice as long as your hair, and tie it around the elastic so that equal lengths are hanging down on either side.

2 Instead of dividing your hair into three sections to plait, use the whole pigtail as one section, and the ends of ribbon as the second and third sections. Start plaiting by crossing one ribbon over the hair to centre, then the other ribbon over to centre then the hair to centre. Keep doing this until you reach the bottom of your hair.

3 Secure the end of the plait (hair and ribbons together) with another tiny elastic. Then wrap the ribbon around either side of the elastic to cover it up, and finish with a cute bow. Do as many of these pretty plaits as you want.

dress it up!

Add another ribbon detail by slipping in these clips at the top of the plait.

Tiny crocodile clips can also help to secure the bottom of the plait.

Try these sparkly dragonfly clips.

Pick a ribbon that's really bright and matches your outfit.

half curly half straight

Can't make up your mind whether to go curly or play it straight? How about half and half? The best thing about this style is that it doesn't matter whether you start with hair that's curly or straight – or anywhere in between – because the end result is a cool mix of both. Plus, depending on what kind of accessories you pick, this half ponytail can go from casual to dressy without a problem!

how to do it

you'll need: brush • gel • curling iron
• hairspray • crocodile clips

1 Rub a small dollop of gel through damp hair, then flip your head upside down and blow dry. When it's dry, flip hair back up and lightly brush. Use a comb to give yourself a centre parting.

2 When the curling iron is hot, wrap a small section of hair around the barrel. Only curl up to ear level – the top should stay straight. Clamp the iron closed and leave for 5 seconds. Release. Repeat on the rest of your head.

3 Spritz your head with hairspray, then pull the front back and clip behind your ears. Be sure to attach the clips right at the beginning of the curls, so hair is smooth above them.

style tip

If your hair is super curly you can skip the curling iron entirely. Instead, start with damp hair and apply gel from the roots and half way down, and then smooth the hair down with a comb. Pin the hair securely behind your ears with combs to keep it super smooth even longer.

dress it up!

This clip can just be slipped in and will hold hair securely behind your ears.

A comb is another alternative to hold hair in place.

A cluster of small clips like this one works just as well as one big clip.

clip it back!

To give this look an even more glamorous and romantic feel, try pulling the front section back loosely and securing it with a pretty clip in the back. Make sure the clip sits loosely to keep the relaxed style.

the**twist**

First we showed you what a cool idea it is to twist up the front of your head, now imagine if you added two twisted pigtails to the mix! That's right, your hair is totally twisted. Depending on the accessories you choose, you can take this style from subtle to far-out just by changing the crocodile clips or adding a flower accessory. We love the twist because it looks complicated, but once you master it, you'll be able to do it in just a few minutes.

how to do it

you'll need: comb • medium crocodile clips • mini crocodile clips • slides • hairspray

1 Start by combing your hair straight back with a wide-tooth comb. Use the comb to create three sections (left, center, and right) and secure each with a medium crocodile clip. Now remove the medium size clip from one of the sections, and pick up about half of the width of this section at the hairline. Start twisting the piece back with your fingers, picking up the hair directly behind it as you go. Secure the twist with a mini crocodile clip.

2 Continue twisting sections until all three big crocodile clips are replaced with cute twists. Next, divide the loose ends between two low bunches in the back, and secure with elastics.

3 Grab one bunch and twist it until it coils around the elastic. Pin it with slides to hold it in place. Do the same to the other side, then spritz your head with hairspray and pat down any stray hairs.

dress it up!

Twist-in gems are a great way to dress up the two twisted buns at the back!

Mini tortoiseshell clips hold twists in place and look great on all hair colours.

Beaded slides dress up your twists with a bit of glitz.

style tip

Girls with a fringe can do this style in a couple of ways: twist your fringe back with the rest of your hair, or let it hang.

wraparound

These over-the-head plaits are totally hip — and cute to boot! They're also so easy to do (after you master the art of plaiting) that you may just find yourself sporting this look the whole week. You can use accessories to make it work for any occassion.

style tip

If your hair is long, you might be able to loop the plaits back and forth over your head. Just tuck the ends under wherever they land.

how to do it

you'll need: brush • comb
• hair elastics • hair slides

1 Brush dry hair to remove any tangles and, using a comb, divide your hair into two equal sections (left and right).

2 Grab the right section of your hair and start plaiting (for details on how to plaits hair, go to Beautiful Plaits on page 34). Be sure not to make plaits too tight – starting about an inch down from the scalp will help. Do the left side the same way.

3 Lift both plaits up and secure them at the top of your head using slides. Tuck the ends under to make it look like you've got one smooth plait going around.

dress it up!

Use a bejewelled slide to attach the plaits at the top of your head.

This flower pin would look great slipped into one of the plaits right above your ear.

Position this butterfly slide to peek out from under plaits for a playful touch.

Twist these hair gems into the plaits for some night-time drama.

glamour**waves**

Learning to curl your hair makes it easy to create lots of new styles – including simple but glamorous waves. These glamour waves look great on everyone, and can be worked into an updo and dressed up for a party, or left to hang down for a fun day of shopping.

how to do it

you'll need: spray gel • comb
• rollers (with pins) • hair spray

1 Lightly spray damp hair with a spray gel from roots to ends. Use a wide-tooth comb to get rid of tangles and distribute the gel evenly. Give yourself a centre parting using the comb. Next, grab a 5-cm square section of hair on the right side of the parting and comb it out again.

2 Grab a hot roller and place it underneath the ends of the 5-cm section. Start rolling toward your scalp. When the roller reaches your scalp, secure it with a slide (unless you have self-sticking Velcro rollers, the pins should be included). Repeat until all hair is rolled up.

3 Leave curlers in for about 10 minutes, or until they are cool. (If you're using Velcro rollers, use your blowdryer to heat the curls.) Remove all the rollers and run your fingers through your hair to loosen the curls into pretty waves. Spritz with hairspray to give your curls extra staying power.

style tip

If you hair is fine and poker straight, spritz the piece of hair that you're about to put in the roller with hairspray beforehand to make sure the curl sticks.

dress it up!

A fancy headband in hot pink and silver sets off this pretty style.

Rhinestones make this clip a dressed-up way to pull curls back for a special occasion.

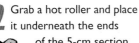

Flowery slides are great for keeping hair out of your face in style.

Try a dark-coloured clip to blend in with brown or black hair in the prettiest way.

crimpedandcool

Are you ready to make waves? If you've never tried this funky style before, then get set to have some fun. Not only is the whole look of crimped hair cool, but it's also a great thing to do with friends. Why not invite some of your girlfriends over during the day and get out the crimping iron? You'll have a wild style for going out to the cinema or to a party.

how to do it

you'll need: leave-in conditioner
• paddle brush • blowdryer • crimping iron

1 Start by spritzing damp hair with leave-in conditioner from roots to ends to help to protect it while you are crimping. Next, flip your head upside down and blowdry. When your hair is dry, brush it to remove any tangles. Plug in your crimping iron to let it warm up.

2 Hold up a small piece of your hair and clamp the crimping iron around it, near the roots. Leave the crimping iron closed for 3–5 seconds, then release. Move the crimper down the hair so the top is just below where the last crimp ended. Be sure to hold the crimper in place for the same amount of time in each place.

3 When you have crimped your whole head, lightly brush your hair once to create a full effect. Spritz your whole head with hairspray to help the crimp last as long as you can.

dress it up!

These slides are great for adding a little colour near your face.

Wear a couple of these clips in a row and add some serious style.

This skinny headband is perfect for pulling out-of-control hair back.

style tip

If you have a fringe, either pull it back in this style or just skip the crimp. A crimped fringe looks totally weird!

These silver crocodile clips sparkle with rhinestones.

clip it up!

Crimped hair can get B-I-G so if it's falling in your face, it's a good idea to clip the front sections back. Start by making a centre parting. Grab a small section of hair from one side and twist it three times before pinning it back above your ear. Do the same with the other side.

Rosie

Nikki

Alexis

Am

How do you wear your hair for special occasions?

Do you have a hairstyle for weddings and dances? What do you do with your 'do for a holiday dinner? Which accessories look best when it's time to get really glammed-up? Need a bit of inspiration? Look no further! This section has party-perfect hair covered with tonnes of cascading curls, sparkly hair accessories and even chopsticks (trust us, they look cool!). Some of these styles are trickier than others, but even girls who can't tell a curling iron from a crimper will find lots of looks that are totally do-able – and totally chic. So, what are you waiting for? It's time to party!

Nierah

ponytail**wrap**

Got a last minute party invite? Whip up this polished look in a flash. While some glam hairdo's take a while to master this pretty ponytail can literally be done in minutes. You can keep it chic and simple or add a little sparkle with your favourite hair accessory. A sparkly slide will look pretty slipped in your hair right at the temples but some cool dangling earrings will also do the trick.

how to do it

you'll need: paddle brush • hair elastic • hair slide

1   Start by brushing your hair and then scooping it back into a low ponytail, leaving a small section of hair from underneath the ponytail out of the elastic.

2   Wrap the loose section of your hair around the elastic until there is only a 2 cm section left. Secure the end underneath the ponytail with a slide.

mix it up!

why not double up?

If one ponytail wrap is good, then two are positively fabulous! Just divide your hair into bunches instad of a ponytail in Step 1. For a cool, futuristic look, try using a bigger piece of hair as the wraparound.

style tip

Hey, fine-haired girls: to avoid taking volume away from your ponytail, keep the wraparound piece pretty skinny. You can also use mousse to plump up your hair before pulling it back in Step 1.

dress it up!

This slide with a star pattern will look great sweeping aside a grown out fringe.

This rounded clip does the wraparound look in an ultra-glittery way.

A pretty comb dresses up the sleek sides of this simple 'do.

These twist-in rhinestones will look great in darker hair.

flip**tail**

A gorgeous party style that only takes a hairbrush and hair elastic? It does exist! This style is so simple you'll wonder why you didn't think of it before. But just because it's easy to master, don't think it's boring. With a few key accessories, you can transform it from funky to romantic to drop-dead gorgeous!

how to do it

you'll need: hair brush • hair elastic

1 Start by brushing dry hair straight back and securing it into a low ponytail with an elastic. Don't have the elastic right at your scalp; make the ponytail a little loose.

2 Use your fingers to make a hole in the hair directly above the elastic (this is why you want it loose).

3 Hold the hole open with one hand while the other hand flips the ponytail under and up through the hole. Smooth your hair into place with your hands, and you're done!

romantic flip

Girls with curly or thick hair can go for this graceful style by keeping the flipped-under ponytail very low and loose. You can also pull out some pieces of hair from the front to frame your face – such a pretty look!

This leather band is ideal for a low ponytail. The stick slides through to keep it in place.

mix it up!

dress it up!

An elastic with rhinestones adds a party flair to hair.

style tip

Girls with straight hair can add a little pizzazz to the Flip Tail by curling the ends of the ponytail with a curling iron.

How great does this leather butterfly look in curly hair? Perfect!

Colourful slides sweep back loose pieces and give this style extra flair.

A beaded hairpin adds sparkle. Just stick it right at the ponytail holder to accent the feature flip.

perfect**pompadour**

Don't you love this look? We think it's cool because it looks 1950's yet modern. Teasing is one of those hair tricks that was massive a few years ago and has now made a comeback. Not only is this look glamorous, it's also flattering to most faces because it adds volume at the top of your head. Go on – grab your comb and be a tease!

dress it up!

A glittery crocodile clip will hold thick hair in place.

how to do it

you'll need: blowdryer • hair elastic • fine-tooth or teasing comb • hair slides • hairspray

1   Start with damp hair and flip your head upside down and blow-dry while scrunching with your hands – don't use a hairbrush. When your hair is dry, flip your head right side up and smooth with your fingers.

2   Gather the side and back of your hair into a loose ponytail that sits in the middle of the back of your head. Leave the top of your hair loose.

3   Take the front of your hair and hold it straight up. With the other hand, place the teeth of the comb at the top of the hair, then drag it to the roots (this is called teasing). Do this a couple of times, then repeat on the rest of the loose section.

4   Next, gather all of the teased sections and pull them back towards the crown of your head. Twist the hair around your finger to create a loose coil. Pin the coil at the crown.

5   Use your fingers to gently lift the hair up at the front (this gives you the pompadour part). When you've pulled it as high as you want to go, lightly comb the top smooth and mist your whole head with hairspray to keep it in place.

This elastic is a glam option for securing finer hair.

Add this clip right behind the pompadour to keep it pouffy and in place.

hang loose!

The pompadour looks equally good on its own, so feel free to skip the ponytail and just leave your hair hanging down.

This elastic with a butterfly attached looks perfect in this pompadour.

style tip

Girls with curls can skip the teasing steps because with all those ringlets you've already got tonnes of volume. Lucky you!

ponytailveil

 If you love to wear your hair down but still want to add a little personality, this style is for you. This style looks sleek from the front and pretty from the back. Also, just like the picture don't be afraid to glam the veil up even more with hair gems.

how to do it

you'll need: hair brush • wide-tooth comb
• 6 small hair elastics

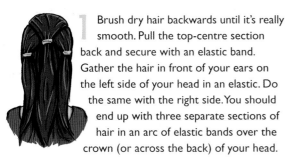

1 Brush dry hair backwards until it's really smooth. Pull the top-centre section back and secure with an elastic band. Gather the hair in front of your ears on the left side of your head in an elastic. Do the same with the right side. You should end up with three separate sections of hair in an arc of elastic bands over the crown (or across the back) of your head.

style tip

If you have fine hair, perhaps try an elastic topped off by a crocodile clip so the veil doesn't slip.

2 Divide the centre ponytail into two sections and connect the right section to the right ponytail using a small elastic. This elastic should sit about two inches below the first elastic.

3 Take the left section of the middle ponytail and connect it to the left ponytail. You will now have two ponytails hanging down. Finally, connect both ponytails into one.

dress it up!

Choose some small crocodile clips in a colour that matches your outfit.

These small sparkly grips will look lovely slipped in right above one of the top ponytails.

This textured elastic is a great option for girls with fine hair as it will really hold the tiny ponytails in place.

Hair gems can be twisted into hair in between the elastics for added glamour.

These jewelled hair pins will work above each elastic for a little shimmer.

These hair jewells snap on just like buttons.

french**plait**

When it comes to French Plaits it seems like everyone falls into one of two categories – those who can do them and those who can't. Well, if you're the latter, we've got you covered because here's the step-by-step on a style that's never out of fashion! The reason we love French Plaits is that once you've got them in, they stay put. Absolutely perfect for a family wedding or anything else that's fun but formal.

style tip
If you want to let your fringe hang loose, just start the plait a little further back on your head.

how to do it
you'll need: hairbrush • wide tooth comb • 2 hair elastics

3 Before crossing the right side to centre again, pick up a piece of hair from outside of the plait so that it becomes part of the righthand section. Then cross the combined section over to centre.

1 Start with dry hair. First, brush to remove any tangles. Make a middle parting from the front of your hair all the way to the back using a wide-tooth comb. Secure one side with an elastic to get it out of the way for now.

4 Next, grab a small piece of hair to the left of the braid and add it to the lefthand section. Cross the combined left section over to centre.

2 Working with the loose side, grab the hair from the front of your head and separate it into three sections. Start by crossing over the sections once like you would a normal plait (check out Low Pigtails on page 34 for instructions).

5 Keep plaiting like this – adding in hair before every cross – until all the loose hair is incorporated into the plait. Continue to the end of your hair with a regular braid and then secure with an elastic. Do the same with the opposite side.

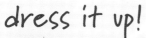

dress it up!

This shiny bauble wraps up braids with a splash of fun.

Why use a plain elastic when you can use this bejewelled one?

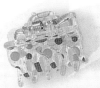

Use mini-clips to pull back shorter pieces that won't stay put in the braid.

Don't you love these colourful and crinkly elastics?

mix it up!

Leave the ends loose to make this style more casual – just stop once you've French plaited down to the hairline and secure hair with a cute ponytail holder. You could also stop the plait halfway (use a clip to hold) and let the bottom half of your hair fall free for a pretty half-up/half-down version.

plaitedbun

 If you've ever spent time in ballet classes, you'll know that this style is perfectly pretty and easy to do. The trick to making this kind of bun flattering is to do it high enough so that you can see it from the front. When a style is as simple and sleek as this one, the only real way to give it personality is with hair accessories, so don't hold back! Twist in some gems or slip in a comb – with this simple style, a few jewels are what will give it personality.

how to do it

you'll need: brush • hair elastic • hair slides

1 Brush dry hair to make sure it's knot-free. Gather all of your hair up into a high ponytail and secure with an elastic.

funky bun

See these gems in her hair? So pretty.

After you've put your hair up in a ponytail, why not create lots of tiny plaits instead of one big one? Just plait as many little ones as you want, then wrap the whole collection around and pin it in place. You can also try twisting the whole bunch first or leaving some loose for different variations on this funky 'do.

mix it up!

dress it up!

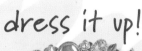

This pink comb will look great slid next to the bun so the teeth point toward its center.

Clip these rhinestone clips right underneath the bun.

Twisty hair gems look fab circling the bun – or in any configuration you can think of!

style tip

Curly girls should start with damp hair to make this style look extra sleek.

2 Divide the ponytail into three sections. Begin plaiting by crossing the right hand section over the middle section and then the left hand section over the middle section. Repeat until you reach the end of your hair.

3 Wrap the plait around the elastic and tuck the end of the braid under the bun. Slide in a bobby pin to secure it. Pin the rest of the plaited bun in place by inserting hair slides all around the base of your bun until it feel secure.

elegantupdo

This elegant hairstyle will really get you noticed! It's perfect for a really special occasion and will bring red-carpet glamour to any dress. For added glitz choose bold and sparkling hair accessories or for a more natural look slide fresh flowers into your hairdo. Whatever accessories you choose, it's a look with real impact.

how to do it

you'll need: paddle brush • hair elastic • hair spray • hair slides • curling iron

style tip

Not everyone's hair holds a curl the same. If yours isn't as curly as you want after five seconds, roll it up in the curling iron again and hold for another five seconds.

1 First, plug in your curling iron. Start the style by brushing dry hair backwards and securing it with an elastic into a high ponytail. Separate out a section of your ponytail – about one sixth of your hair.

2 Spritz the small section with hair spray and wrap it around your finger to create a loose coil. Then use a hair slide to pin the coil to the base of the ponytail.

3 Separate another small section right next to the pinned up piece. Spritz with hair spray to get it ready to curl. Then open the curling iron and wrap the hair around the barrel. Close the iron and hold for five seconds. Spritz with hair spray again to help set the curl.

4 Alternate between pinning coiled sections down and curling sections until the entire ponytail is done. If you want more curly tendrils, you can curl the sections around your face as well. At the end, spritz your whole head with one final mist of hair spray.

dress it up!

Small sparkly twists pack a big glam impact tucked between loops.

Try sticking this bejewelled pin in right next to the ponytail.

This butterfly elastic loops around your ponytail to give you glitz from the outset.

A pretty comb pushed underneath the bun gives a ballerina look.

mix it up!

up in a bun

For a gorgeous variation of this updo, skip Step 3 and repeat Step 2 until all the pieces of your ponytail are looped and pinned like the first. You can create an even more intricate look by using smaller pieces of the ponytail. Be sure to choose occasion-appropriate accessories to complete the look.

simply**beautiful**

This style is truly fit for a princess. It's chic, classic, and the perfect 'do to show off a fabulous clip. Since this look is all about learning how to do a pro-quality blowdry, it might take a couple of tries to master. Trying to hold a blowdryer in one hand and the brush in the other may feel a little awkward at first, but after a while it will become second nature – and you'll look Simply Beautiful!

how to do it

you'll need: straightening balm or cream
• wide tooth comb • 6 hair clips • blowdryer
• round brush • paddle brush • shine spray • large clip

1 Start with damp hair. Massage a medium-sized dollop of straightening cream through your hair from roots to ends. Comb your hair to remove tangles, then use the comb to make a side parting from the crown of your head forwards. Divide your hair into six sections (three top and three bottom), twisting and clamping each section with a crocodile clip.

2 Section by section, begin blowdrying your hair. Use a round brush on the underside of the section, pulling it down from roots to tips with the hairdryer blowing right above it. Repeat this on every section until your hair is smooth and dry.

3 Spritz your hair with shine spray and brush it. Grab a section of your hair from the front (a little smaller than the width of your forehead) and pull straight back. Brush until it's really smooth, then clip the section a couple of inches back.

dress it up!

This tortoiseshell clip is perfect if you want to sport this style at school.

If you hair is fine, a comb is another option for holding it back.

This rhinestone clip is another way to add some glitter to your look.

style tip

If your hair is kinky curly, save yourself the muscle power. It takes a professional to blowdry real ringlets straight.

add some curls

If you've got straight hair, it looks pretty to add some curls to the ends of your hair with this style. (Follow Step 3 from the Elegant Updo on page 80 to master the curling iron.) When you've finished, spritz your hair with hairspray to make sure your new curls last.

pick-upsticks

Look totally original (and utterly hip) by putting chopsticks to a new use. This crafty style adds Asian flair to your hair with delicious results! Add dressed-up sticks to an already cute bun for a look that's perfect for going to a friend's birthday party or out on the town.

how to do it

you'll need: brush • hair elastic • hair slides • wax • hair sticks

1 Start by brushing dry hair to get rid of any tangles.

2 Flip your head upside down and pull your hair into a high ponytail. Secure with an elastic.

3 Twist the ponytail into a tight coil, then twist it around the elastic to create a bun. Secure the bun with plenty of slides (but make sure you leave a few ends sticking out).

4 To finish your look, rub some wax into the ends so that it looks spiky. Stick two sticks in an X formation into the bun.

dress it up!

These sticks that are touched with gold are perfect for a dressy occasion.

Sticks in bright pink will work on any hair shade.

These wavy sticks will look great on blondes or redheads because of their dark colour.

style tip

Hair too short for bun? Try doing a mini-bun with the top half of your hair. Just use smaller sticks so they don't overpower your style.

french**twist**

The French Twist is a classic – always glamorous and beautiful. But just because this is a timeless technique it doesn't mean your 'do will look stuck in the Dark Ages. What keeps our version modern and fabulous is its funky loosened-up style. Let hair stick out of the top in a cute sprout and pull some loose pieces down to frame your face. Tres Chic!

how to do it

you'll need: brush • hairspray • hair slides • wax

1 Lightly mist dry hair with hairspray before gathering it in the back of your head as if you were going to do a low ponytail.

2 Start twisting your hair while pulling it upwards at the same time (the ends of your hair should be pointing to the ceiling). Keep coiling until only the ends of your hair are sprouting out.

3 Insert hair slides all the way up the coil to hold everything in place.

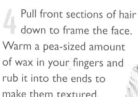

4 Pull front sections of hair down to frame the face. Warm a pea-sized amount of wax in your fingers and rub it into the ends to make them textured.

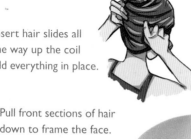

long and loose

Instead of spiky ends, try winding them around to make a loose bun at the top of the twist. This modification looks great with curls – pull a few strands of hair out of the back and sides.

Use a glam hair slide to put curls just where you want them.

style tip

Girls with thicker hair look great in this style. Just be sure to use lots of slides to keep everything in a twist!

dress it up!

Insert this butterfly hair pin right above the updo.

Clip any stray front sections back with this rhinestone clip.

With a giant crocodile clip, this style goes from glamorous to casual.

sleeksidebun

When is a bun not a bun? When it kicks to the side for a whole new take on sleek! This style is flattering because from the front, you'll see the bun poking out from one side, so it's a little less severe than the usual kind. Plus, this is a simple way to change a hairstyle that you may already know how to do but didn't know how to update.

how to do it

you'll need: brush • wide-tooth comb • hair elastic • shine spray

1 Brush dry hair to remove tangles. Use a wide-tooth comb to create a side parting. Gather your hair into a low ponytail on the opposite side of the parting.

This flower pin will stay secure if you push the teeth of it into the bun.

mix it up!

make it messy

You can also take this style and make it look a bit more edgy by following the steps for a Messy Ponytail on page 20, then coming back to steps 3, 4 and 5 from Sleek Side Bun.

style tip

Got curls? Make the bun a little looser for a softer style – or add some shine spray before you twist up into the sleeker version.

dress it up!

A shimmery comb can tuck right into the top of the bun.

You'll look pretty in pink with this clip-and-bun cover-up combo.

Rows of rhinestones will light up your look! Try a pair of these for special occasions.

2 Twist the ponytail tightly until it starts to coil up, then wind it loosely into a bun. Secure the bun by sticking in slides from all sides of the bun (if you feel them cross over, that's great because your hair will really stay in place).

3 Lightly mist your whole head with a shine spray and clip in a hair decoration with some sparkle.

curlycue

Looking for a style that's perfect for a party but still loose and carefree? This is it. It's a great way for girls with curls to showcase their ringlets and lots of fun if your hair is straight. You can create curls with the right curling iron and a little hairspray. Romantic ringlets falling over your shoulders look pretty and bohemian.

how to do it

you'll need: spray gel • comb • rollers (with pins) • hairspray • hair elastic • hair slides • curling iron

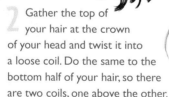

1 Start by curling hair into Glam Waves by following the instructions on page 64. When you're done, create a side parting with a comb.

2 Gather the top of your hair at the crown of your head and twist it into a loose coil. Do the same to the bottom half of your hair, so there are two coils, one above the other.

3 When placing the hair slides to secure each coil, be sure to keep them very loose – three or four slides for each one should do the trick.

4 To finish the look, use lots of decorative hair accessories to pin the curls where you want them. Be sure to leave a couple of pieces loose to frame your face.

hippie chick

Give this bohemian style more of a hippie look by adding some Baby Plaits (page 34) randomly throughout the style. Secure them with tiny elastics or crocodile clips.

Be bold with bright mini crocodile clips.

dress it up!

Stick this flower pin in your hair so it looks like it's tucked behind your ears.

A hair slide with a dangling jewel will look lovely clipping up a curl.

style tip

Straight-haired girls will definitely want to use a curling iron on the sections around your face.

glossary

Blowdryer: A styling tool that uses hot, pressured air to dry, with the aid of a round brush, to straighten hair. Some models also have a cold setting that blasts cool air to set curls.

Brush (round): A brush that has bristles all the way around the top. Best used for blowing hair straight or curling the ends of your hair.

Brush (paddle): A brush that has a flat top with bristles on one side. Best used for brushing out tangles on dry hair.

Chignon: A classic French term for a type of updo. It's always at the back of your head is a very smooth and sleek version of a bun.

Comb (wide-tooth): This kind of comb has big gaps between the teeth, which makes it ideal for combing damp hair.

Comb (fine-tooth): A usually plastic styling tool with very small teeth set close together; best for finishing touches like smoothing down stray hairs or making a precise part.

Conditioner (regular): A creamy moisturizing product used after shampoo. Can be applied to full hair shaft for normal hair, or just to ends for oily hair.

Conditioner (leave-in): A light cream or spray added to damp hair after showering. Great for dry hair, and also as a protective layer before using heated styling tools.

Crimping Iron: A V-shaped styling tool with two metal plates that create a zig-zag form when clamped together. Used to create a frizzy style.

Crown: The part of your head that at the top but in the back. This is a flattering place to put high ponytails and buns, since you can see the style from the front and the back.

Curling Iron: A barrel-shaped heated styling tool that hair wraps around to set in a curl. Available in small, medium, and large widths for tight or loose curls.

French Twist: A classic style in which hair is pulled back, twisted upward, and pinned in place.

Gel: A sticky styling product that works best to add volume to roots or hold hair in place for a complicated updo. Best applied to damp hair for firm hold.

Hairpins: Metal styling pins shaped like a narrow U for securing loose pieces of hair in updos. Available in natural colors to blend in to hair.

Hair Slides: Metal pins used to hold pieces of hair tightly in place or help hold an updo securely. Available in different colors to blend in with various hair colors, or with decoration such as gems, flowers, or colours.

Hairspray (aerosol): A dry styling product that comes in a can and is sprayed on in a fine mist to give hair a final hold after styling.

Hairspray (pump): A wet styling product that is sprayed onto hair in a mist. Best used with heated styling aids, which will dry the spray for extra holding power.

Mousse: A light, creamy styling aid with drying ingredients, great for creating lift. Best applied near roots with fingers or a wide-tooth comb.

Pompadour: A '50s-style hairdo in which the front was combed back into a pouf and the sides and back were very slick.

Rollers (Hot): Heated styling aids that come on a base with metal heating rods sticking out. The rods heat the rollers, which can then be fixed in hair with pins to set soft curls.

Rollers (Velcro): Non-heated rollers with Velcro teeth to hold their place in hair without pins. A blowdryer is needed to heat and set the style.

Scrunching: A way to add volume and texture to hair by balling up a handful of hair and squeezing it with your fingers.

Shampoo: A cleansing product for hair. Should be used every day or every other day in a formula designed for your hair type.

Straighteners: A heated styling tool that uses two flat metal plates to iron hair straight.

Straightening Cream or Balm: A lotion-like styling aid used to help hair dry straight and protect against heat damage from heated styling aids.

Teasing: A technique for adding pouffy volume to hair. A fine-tooth comb is used to brush hair backwards into loose tangles.

Wax: A hard styling product similar to pomade but less greasy. Good for making ends spiky or adding definition and separation to ringlets.

index

Acknowledgements

The publisher would like to thank the following for their kind cooperation in the preparation and production of this book:

The fabulous models: Sakura Akiyama-Bowden, Brittany Barbone, Andrea Bloom, Tess Brokaw, Amy Cacciatore, Alexis Carmody, Michelle Chionchio, Mary-Kate Duffy, Kelsey Evenson, Rosie Fodera. Hannah Gross, Nierah Jinwright, Sade Johnson, Maghee Kelsall, Sade Johnson, Juliette Lam, Nikki Lam, Francesca Lobbe, Juliana Merola, Kristin Molinari, and Autumn Stiles…and also their parents, who stuck with us so very patiently at the photo shoot.

Our amazing hairstylists: Azad Desmeropian, Shukran Dogan, Catherine McDermott, Rhondalyn Roberts, John Lisa, and Angela Woodley, for their wonderful skill and dedication.

The super stylists: Maria Stefania Vavylopoulou and Shima Green, for out-fitting the girls in the coolest clothes.

Thanks also to Josephine and Katherine Yam at Colourscan for their hard work in bringing it all together; to Nanette Cardon for her work on the index; and of course to the always-glamorous Angela Coppola, Donna Mancini, Cristina Clemente, Nichole Morford, Sharon Lucas, and Gregor Hall for all their help and support.

Hair products used in this book included these products from the L'Oréal Studio Line: Crystal Wax, Out of Bed Whipped Gel, Mega Mousse, Mega Gel, Fast Forward, and Finishing Spray.